Dreams

Dreams

Rimple Joshi

authorHOUSE®

AuthorHouse™
1663 Liberty Drive
Bloomington, IN 47403
www.authorhouse.com
Phone: 1-800-839-8640

Published by AuthorHouse   27/08/2012

ISBN: 978-1-4772-2358-1 (sc)
ISBN: 978-1-4772-2359-8 (e)

For my mum Sudha Joshi for always believing in me
and Pankaj my inspiration to move forward.

Dreams
Dreams are not dreams
Without an inspiration to live
To have a goal, a target to complete
I wish I could tell you what I need,
I ask myself questions, awaiting the answers
I hear myself saying . . . .
Keep dreaming as it's only the beginning.

As the white clouds cover the bright blue sky
I feel you holding me tight
The rain falls from the sky
As my tears down my face run dry
I desire a world so unique
But reality is something I hate to feel.

Your love for me is all I need to live and to love in this lonely world
For god only knows
What life would really bring
If my darling you were not with me.

As you close your eyes and fall asleep
I sit alone staring at your face
For if you awake
This moment will pass
So forever I hold you in my thoughts.

A splash of colour
A warmth of happiness
A desire to live is what you bring
Your existence in my life is like a meadow full of roses.

A sudden ache of the heart
A sudden blister of the wind
I hear myself crying
But the tears are nowhere to be found.

The wind on the trees
Makes me shiver from within my soul
I gaze at the moon in the darkness of the night,
Only to find a thorn stuck in my heart.

A moment without you is like a lifetime deprived of water
A thrust so quenching that my eyes imagine you
Beside me holding me without depriving me.

A future, a lifetime or just a moment,
I cherish each moment with you like a never ending fantasy.
Wishing, dreaming, believing there will be more
You make my life, my presence, my existence worth while for
without you
In my heart, mind and soul
I do wonder where I would be
I truly love you more then words can say . . . .
If in this lifetime I am not yours
I promise I will return life after life until we are one.

I love you so much it hurts
Love is all in people yet it never dies
Love is much in winning but is more in losing
Love is ever true yet is ever lying
Love does doubt in liking but is mad in hatred
Love indeed is everything yet indeed is nothing?

Lonely lover you left me to cry
Without a shoulder
I want to know why?
Lonely lover I needed your love to
Gain the respect which I deserved
Lonely lover what did I do wrong to gain such
a horrible curse?
Lonely lover I love you so much
Lonely lover what was the cause.

Your love was so precious to me I thought of you day and
night
And yet you still didn't care,
I loved you for all the love I needed but you still stayed the
same
I thought of you as a great person,
But you just turned out rotten
I always thought you loved me not as much but more then
I loved you
But I was wrong!
I was wrong to have chosen you to step in to my life
If then I heard the cry I would have known you weren't my
type
I still love you with all my heart and soul
But what good is it now when you are someone's love
I hope you really love her not as much but more then you
loved me
I hope it's someone lucky that deserves you more then me and
not somebody who will be thrown.
Still in love but in shock
The precious love keeper.

I gave you my heart, you took away my soul
I gave you my hand you took away my whole body
I felt innocent
Had you committed a crime?
I was sorry you were glad
I felt sick you felt good
I felt ashamed but you felt cool
What had happened no one knew.

Holding your hand, feeling you there
Giving a kiss showing we share
Asking you out knowing the yeah
Feeling secure while your there.

Living without you oh my love
I dare to say how life would be
When every night I cry for you
And every day is just so long
I miss you more and more each day
As every day that passes by
I wonder where you are right now
As thoughts of you are on my mind.

I wake up in the morning and my eyes die to see you
My lips die to touch you
My arms die to hold you
My heart has so many sorrows
I wake up in the morning and wonder how lucky I am to have
you.

Love, love, love
I love you so much
I wonder what went wrong
I asked for a favour it feels like a guilt
I understood you
But you never understood me
Love, love, love
If only you loved

I was and still am unknown to him
The one I love and only shall
What shall I do to tell him now?
God only knows my true fear.

Never fall in love
Your heart has this sudden ache
Jealousy makes you burn inside like a volcano
You think why? Why me?
Why did it have to happen to me?
Your tears full of water turn to tears full of blood
Never fall in love
How did I end up falling in it.

I don't think seeing you was mistake
I think it was more of a nightmare
A nightmare that will haunt me
For the rest of my life.

No matter how hard I try
I cant stop thinking of you
My mind travels so fast as the only
thought it has is of you
My eyes cry for you day and night
As they cant see enough of you
As you're the only one I want.

The smile you give
The tender kiss we share
Just all feels to good to be true
I sit in your arms thinking I'm in deep sleep
Everything you say and do makes life a better place to be.

You and only you why?
When you touch your lips against mine
When you hold me in your arms so tight
When you look in to my eyes so deep
When we share a moment of passion
When we feel so close we cant let go
I feel it in my heart to let you know
I love you more and more.

Only you!
Beneath the wonderful green grass
Above the light blue sky
Between this is nature's beauty
My darling you that makes it a better place
The presence of you
The moment your there
Means so much to the heart, I can't say.

If only!
The pain the hurt wanting you there
Without you so much to handle
The loneliness of no one to share with
The only happiness a life inside me
The freshness of our love
Like a garden full of roses
The friendship we had
The love we shared
Is no longer mine
The pain the hurt
Wanting you there
But knowing it's a little too late.

Awake me from my dreams
Like you've never done before
Touch me like you use to as I can't remember how
Open my heart as you're the only one with the key
Cherish these memories with only me
For memories are more then words that they seem.

The fear of your tear
The sorrows that caused the fatal heart
The moments of happiness
All washed away with grief
The love in my heart that is now at ease.

When the stars shine deep in the sky
I think of my love for you
So strong so deep I wonder why?
When the stars shine deep in the sky
I think how to begin to tell you
Tell you my love is all for you.

Just a few words to say
What I've really wanted to say
Beneath the ground above the sky
Between the sweetness of the air
Between the tender love and care
We share a love so deep and true
That only we shall know is true.

Dreams
Dreaming of a world with you in my arms
Dreaming of a sound so sweet to the ear
Dreaming of a touch so soft and smooth
Dreaming . . . . You awake me
It's true.

A friendship so true
A friendship unreal
A friendship I knew would last forever
The way you spoke
The way you understood
The way it hurts when I hurt you to.

The heat in your heart
Like a volcano erupting
The coldness in your arms
Like the rain is falling
The tears on your cheek
Like the world is breaking

You threw me away without a moment of love
You hurt me so bad without a moment of trust
You left me alone without a shoulder or soul
You broke my heart in pieces that are still unknown.

The tears we once shared
The softness in your face
The sorrows in my eyes
The touch of your lips against mine
The laughter we shared
The happiness the faded
The long nights without you
The thought that you cared has all disappeared
What remains are my tears alone.

The hurt you caused the tears you gave
Will always be there for years to stay
The way you hurt me will remain in the heart
As the tears you gave were truly unreal.

When I sit in your arms beneath the light blue sky
When you touch my soft skin I feel your mine
When you hold me so tight I don't know why
When you whisper in my ear that you're only mine
When we sit so close I can feel the heat
When your lips meet mine I feel so shy
We've come so close we just don't know why?

The lose of you so close to the heart
The moments we shared
The times we were hurt
The failure in our lives that kept us together
Until I noticed you were with another.

Beyond the moon among the stars
Deep in the sky shines the power of love
This is the only way we will know
The love we share the depth of passion
Which shall only be known to us.

Seeing you caused an effect to the heart
Touching you caused a current through my body
Holding you caused me never to let go
Kissing you caused me happiness that was truly unknown.

Love in the heart and no one to share with
Warmth in my arms and no one to hold
Passion in my thoughts and no one to have it
So closer so deep in my every thought.

An amazement or a dream so wonderful that it seems
The words spoken that sounded so sweet
I never knew how much you could love me
Till I saw in your eyes so deep
The need of you wanting me
The happiness awaiting
I could see in your eyes and I knew what to believe.

My memories of you so far from the heart
A moment I regret which I'm glad will never be back
The childhood love that was never there
Not a drop of love in your lonely heart
You deny I am yours and I try and forget it all
The things that you said the hurt that was caused
The small times of happiness, that were covered by hurt
The violence the beating the hatred you caused
Knowing you never cared enough to love
The attention the advice that ever child seeks
Was not given
As you were in a dream
A dream so hurtful you lost your sleep
Your friends, your family even soul it seems
People that thought you loved and cared.
You now live a life . . . .
ALONE
With out a soul by your side.

When I look at you and you look at me I feel there's
a need for me to live
never thought never knew life would be this wonderful
when I look at you I realize my love for you
I love you so much and always will
Never thought never knew
I could love u this much for true.

Dreams aren't just dreams as you feel what you dream
A person so close yet you want him to keep
Feeling a dream that will never come true
Wanting a sharing your ever thought
A dream so unreal
A dream so untrue
It was only a dream that will never come true.

My memories and yours
Written down as feeling of love
Placed in a heart of gold
To cherish for years to go
So among all the lovers in the world
Everybody will know what I done for you
All alone!

When I look at you
I see the love in your heart for me
Never thought never knew
You could love me for true
When I look at you
I feel a warmth surrounding my arms
Wanting to hold you
Never thought never knew
I could feel this close to you
When I look at you
You gaze in to my big brown eyes
Hold me close and ask me why?
I love you so much as it burns you hot from inside
Never thought never knew
That love could be so true.

When you looked at me
I felt an arrow through my heart
So much hurt so much pain
Only no scar to prove my pain
I knew that look meant nothing more then something I had,
had before
I felt the pain so hard it hurt
I felt the blood dripping down my top
As I placed my hand close to my heart
There was nothing there but my past.

A sense of love
A sense of happiness
So close to the heart
Yet still unknown
All I wanted was a bit of love
All I wanted was a bit of happiness
Life has played a joke with me
Living a life has ruined my life
If only I had answers
If only I knew
If only I could have my happiness wioth you.

To live a dream
To fulfill a wish
All seems like a fairy tale
A dream, a wish if only wished hard for
Will become mine forever
A sense of love
Knowing and believing what is truly
In the heart
Never thought would be so difficult.

Your eyes
When I look in to your eyes
I wish you could hold me tight
Whisper in my ear you'll love me forever
But when I looked in to your eyes and told you
I love you forever
You stopped me
Saying we can't have that for real.

The tears from my eyes
Like a never ending nightmare
To live and to dream
A world without all that
Is it destiny or reality?
To wake up from this nightmare and to say
I'm so happy I don't want to cry.

Love me like you've never loved another
Kiss me like you've never kissed another
Hold me forever like a never ending fantasy
Live with me and cherish with me each moment
Like were meant to be.

You stood beside me
And made me smile through my sorrows
You taught me to live without the three letter word
For love is nothing but just a tiny thought from the heart.

We grieve over your loss
As a friend you were close
Never thought never knew
Life would play such a joke with you
You were full of joy
You were full of happiness
And that was really you
You always said you'd be first
But we didn't expect that you would leave us
We feel the pain and wish we'd been there.

The man that once made me smile
I sent away with sadness forever
Reflecting on his face
Like a never ending shadow
Surrounding each inch of his heart
Like forever touching his soul
I wonder were I'd be if I hadn't learnt to smile
For now I realize as all I have is thoughts of him by my side
For the time has disappeared but the memories remain
Both in my heart and his it shall stay
But if only he'd left with a smile on his face
I'd live with a smile on my face to
The man that once made me smile
I sent away with sadness forever.

The house on the hill
Broken as if only a dream
The words the touch the depth
Of passion all feel asleep
You seem to have forgotten
I'm only a person
Who lives a life so painful
You don't seem to feel
The hurt the pain
If only you could feel
You'd sense my tears
Running down your face for real.
When you touched me for the last time
I felt this urge to hold you close
And tell you
That if only you wanted
I could hold you forever
Love you and cherish you
Give you my days and my nights
And make you the happiest man alive

Hunny it's you and only you
And nothing more in life
That makes me happier
Then being with you
The time I spent with you
I feel no pain
You're the happiness that covers
All my pain
For if you were not with me
Life would not be worth living.

You mean more then you think
If only I could tell you
If only I could show
That life is nothing without you
A day in my life will never pass by
Where I won't think of you?

How will I ever say good bye to you
When I look in to your eyes and
Hope you'll stare at me forever
When I'll hear your heart beating
I'd want it to beat along side mine
When I'll sense your lips against mine
I will hear a cry
For don't let me go
Because your love is all I have to live a life.

I walked down the road
At a speed I only know
To sense and to feel a shadow
Only I don't see it on the ground
I build up my speed
As I hear a screech
I look behind
As I'm covered with blood
And I hit the ground.

I once dreamt a dream
To be by your side
To love and to cherish you
In my every thought
Till the day that I die.

I dreamt a dream so deep and true
That I wish for it to come true
You looked in to my eyes so deep
And told me
I will love you
Till the day that I die.

I gazed in to your eyes
And felt you wanted to be mine
You held me tight
Looked in to my eyes
And said hunny
I'm yours forever, by your side.

You may be far away
But I remember you every day
As I close my eyes and hold my ears tight
I feel the beat of your heart
Close to mine.

I'd wish to be with you
Forever in your arms
Like your shadow on the ground
Never to escape
Never to fade away
We'd guide each other
Through the path of love.

I cherished a moment
A thought a desire
That although this is as great as it could be
I could never have it beside me to last me a lifetime.

An angel was sent to cover
My scars from deep within my heart
Were the sadness lay,
With a pinch full of love
He gave me so much happiness that
He made me the person I am

Happiness so unknown
Lying so low, it seems in the ground
To feel and to see
If not a spark a little glimpse
To reach out and say
Come back you're my only hope.

Tempted!
You were so tempted in spending the rest of your life with me
That you couldn't see the problems rising
I felt this urge when you looked at me and told me that is you could
You would hold me, treasure me and spend the rest of your life with me.

A spilt second
Is all I asked from you
For me to show you my love for you
The moments are passing
The days are drifting
There just doesn't seem to be time to tell you for a spilt second
How much I really love you.

For the first time I feel
If I had the power
I'd keep you beside me forever
To love you, to cherish you
To give you all the happiness
Hold you in my arms so close and whisper in your ear
I will love you forever.

A moment of truth
Without ever casting eyes upon you
You looked away and said
If you'd met me before then
We would have truly been a pair.

One day left
Without a moment of hurt
No happiness in the air
As your presence fades away
I dare to see, I dare to realize
That this is it and it will never be
For you and me were just a dream not reality.

The raining falling from the sky
Like the tears from my eyes
Never to stop as I see a puddle
I fear I will drown for all I want
Is to be in your arms
So hold me tight
With the warmth of your arms
And I will live without crying and
The fear of drowning forever.

Forever hold me tight
And never let me out of your sight
I feel this pain
I feel this loneliness
For without you life is nothing
But a day that just passes by.

I want you to hold me tight
Whisper you will love me forever
And share with me the memories
You'd never shared with another.

You came in to my life
Saying why don't you understand
I shred a tear but you didn't even feel a
shiver.

I spent a lifetime loving you
But did not receiver anything back
But tears, sadness and grief all the
way till the last day I was alive.

A sense of hurt so deep in the heart
Yet nobody hears my cry
I just hold my heart and weep quietly
Without anybody hearing a sound.

Yet again!
I knew you'd step back in to my life and ruin
Everything I had gained
But you will not stop me
And I will go on
Leaving you so far behind.

You looked in to my eyes so deep
I just knew you craved to say
That if it was up to you
You would have taken me away.

Good night and sweet dreams my darling
As special as you make my days
I wish I could make your life time that happy
Give you my days and my nights
Give you my heart and my soul
But most of all give you all the love in the world.

Without a moment of hesitation
Without seeing my tears
You caused so much pain unintentionally
That you caused the heart to fail.

You threw me away without the feeling of love
You washed me away like a fantasy on a boat
I lost my purpose of living or feeling and sat there alone
Picking up my hearts pieces.

I once told you
That the time would come
Were you shall learn to know
The people that loved you
The people that cared
The people that were truly your friends
You now regret
What your past caused your presence and
Nobody knows what the future holds.

Why do I feel
This amazement in my heart
That the tears I shred
When I wept in my loneliness
Will never happen again
Its your tears now
To weep and to feel what I felt
Now maybe you will know
Maybe you will feel
What I had once felt
When you had left me all alone.

I sat in your arms
Sensing your essence in my beauty
Without a sudden shiver
I felt my heart beating faster then ever.

You caused me nothing but pain
From deep within my heart
I felt a tear falling
So strong, so deep
I heard it as it hit the ground
I felt the ground opening
As it buried me in its arms
I felt an urge to be without you
Cause below in the ground
Meant more to me then being in your arms.
Once I wished upon a star
I didn't know what I wanted
All I wished for was happiness
In one big bundle I got
You bought a life time of happiness
Happiness I'd never felt before
You made me smile, you made me laugh
But most of all you made me feel special
In your own unique way you made me feel loved
I didn't know what I'd do without you
Until you broke my heart.

The white clouds cover the dark sky
As if to remind me that your holding me tight
The night falls the moon shines
I see a face appear in the sky
I look with amazement to see your face appear
With the stars shinning and the moon glowing
All I want is you beside me.

My wish, my dream
My inspiration to live
All broken down in one spilt second
My eyes, my lips my heart cry for justice
The thought that I could never love again
That thought that you will never be mine
My wish, my dream that will never be true
My life time will go without happiness and that true.

You are my reason to live
My reason to smile
My reason for happiness
Without you life is nothing at all
I gave you everything
All for a pinch full of love
Although you never even gave me that
Not even when I asked
You took away my happiness
You left me with scars
Just by saying you don't love me enough.

My dream to wake up in your arms
To hold you tight and never let go
To close my eyes and hear your heart
To love you like crazy
So you never let me go.

When I placed that ring on your finger
I knew it had to be forever
You chose not to love me
You chose not to be faithful
But how could I hate you when you touched my heart.

My dying wish!
To place my memories, my happiness
In my heart to hold it tight and lay down
To take it away and remember it forever
I dreamt a dream that will never come true
I knew in my heart it was untrue
I craved for the love
I wanted the attention
As I lay down to think
I wasn't there it was only my soul.

The empty closet
Like the lover in my heart
Has shown what was truly in your heart
The space that will never be filled
The hope that you will wake from this dream
All lies empty
In your empty closet.

The angel in the sky
Smile at my grave
As if to tell me
Sorry you lived a lie.

As the minutes pass by on the clock
the days pass by,
the months pass by
I hope years don't go by
As the minutes pass on the clock
All I wish for is my love by my side
If only I could bring the days and months
Back change it all and ask you why?
Tell you all I want to hear is
I love you till the day that I die.

Dreaming of a world
So simple yet so true
A depth of passion
Deep in the heart
Warmth surrounding every aspect
Of my life
A sense of happiness
Yet so unknown
Deep within the feeling I share all alone.

The most beautiful thing
To sense love in the heart
Every time the wind blows by me
I sense your presence around me
The soft touch, as if you're touching me
holding me.
Telling me that although we are not together
You haven't left me completely.

One day you will realize, you will learn
What true love is all about
When you get hurt
When you will cry
That one day you will remember
You put me through the same.

The days pass by and as night falls
The clouds disappear as if the darkness
Is holding the clouds tight
To cover the whiteness in the sky
I dream of a night where you hold me tight

I sit here and think and wonder
to myself.
Why have I gone so heartless?
Why don't I ever cry?
I think of all the things and believe
This is what you made me and I ask myself why?

The sudden tear
As if to hit the ground
To say the world has broken down
Without you by my side
It's going to be hard to heal.

With hopes and dreams
That seem so close
I hold my hand on my heart
Swear to god a vow I want
To live a dream forever
For without you
My world, my dream
My inspiration to live
Might just die as hopes and dreams.

An amazement or a dream
Side by side I'm holding you tight
To hold you forever
To wrap my dreams, my desires
To live, to cherish, my memories and
then die peacefully.
When I see the stars twinkling in the sky
I remember the twinkle you bring in my eyes
You fill the darkness in my life
Like a star deep in the sky
You shine a ray of light
With a tiny star, that your like.

The ground beneath my feet
Shattered in a instance
Which dropped to a depth?
that was unreal,
the pieces were broken
both my heart and his
you could never really make it one
it was all but a dream.

When the sun shines and
the birds sing in the blue sky
I hear a sweet sound to the ear
That reminds me that you're near.

The moments we have
The laughter we share
All seems unreal like a
Dream in my sleep
I don't want to wake
As I have a sudden ache
So deep in the heart
As if I get woken
I will just fade.

The mystery man
The day I met him
I felt a shiver through my spine
So warm, so sudden
It'd been so long since I felt
I dint know his feeling for me
Yet I looked in his eyes and saw
The world beneath my feet.

So painful as it struck the heart
Like a hundred arrows placed in
One wound hit so hard the heart had shattered in pieces
So small, they were scattered.
At such a speed the sudden ache
Became a broken part of my fatal heart.

The helpless heart
When I look at you and
Gaze in to your eyes
I see a world so wonderful
It seems.
I dare to feel, a feeling so true
For the thought of happiness
Deep within the heart just feels untrue
For the helpless heart.

The bleeding heart
With all the memories
Of happiness and sadness
My bleeding heart speaks out aloud
my heart has so many sorrows
but I dare to show the world
the depth of hurt, the broken heart
nobody to love, nobody to care
the bleeding heart is hurting hard
to cherish the happiness
to forget the sadness
is all a dream, that can not be done.

Memories will remain memories
And nothing more
I hold on to your thoughts forever
Wonder what had happened
I asked myself a question unknown
Yet do not have an answer
I feel my memories will remain memories
even when I'm gone.

When I look in to your eyes and
See no answer of mine
I have a thought so deep in
The heart that I really wish
I could show you, tell you
I'm truly the one for you.

When you hold me in your arms so tight
When you whisper sweet things,
I don't know why?
I sense a thought from deep within
That your telling me that your all mine.

The tears from my eyes that feel at such a speed
Like the sadness that surrounded my life
Like the loneliness that was by my side.

The sadness in my heart
The sorrows in my eyes
The whole world is breaking
In front of my eyes
I dare to look beneath me
As I wonder what I'll see
As the world is breaking
As my sadness is fading.

The happiness that surrounded the day
Like memories that had been left behind
The thought of laughter to fill the walls was
filled with tears alone.
You now come along, to give a smile to us all
Without realizing its to late now.

When you look at me and gaze in to my eyes
When we sit so close, you're holding me tight
When your lips meet mine, I feel so shy
When you touch me so softly, I want to ask you will you be
mine?

The moonlight glowing in the sky
As if to foam a shadow of some kind
Is it an amazement or is it just a dream?
You're standing by the moonlight it seems.

You broke my heart
without a moment of love
you shattered my dreams
like a mirror hitting the ground
I lost my image
You took away my identity
All I was left with was me
Shattered in pieces.
Without ever knowing
What happiness really is
I sit here today
With a smile on my face
Knowing and believing
Life can only be what I make it.

I wish you could tell me
That you do really love me
From the top of your head
To the bottom of your toe
All you want is me and n nothing more at all.

How will I ever forget?
As you lay in my arms
And close your eyes
As you hold me so tight
And then I ask you why?
You look in to my eyes
As I whisper I love you
You mumble a humble
But never tell me
What the heart truly feels.

When I look at you
I have this urge to tell you
That if there was nothing else
But me and you
I'd worship you and treasure you
And spend every moment with you
Like a never ending fantasy.

A moment lost
Without a memory left
All because of you
As you once said
That you've never felt
A feeling or an emotion
Not even closeness
To my heart or my soul.

If I were an angel in the sky
I'd spread my wings and shine above you
Like the stars in the sky
To give you all the happiness
to last you a lifetime.

I saw an angel in the sky
But did not know how to feel
I had an urge to spread my wings
And fly really high
I saw the clouds floating by
Only to realize I was still standing
And you were by my side.

My empty bottle
That seems empty with air
Is full of memories
That scare me to death
I dare to open
The empty bottle
For all it is
Is a bottle of sorrows.

How do I live in the presence
When all the future holds
Are memories and questions?
From the past, that haunt me
Every second of each day

Every time I look at you
I remember how much I hurt you
You say you have forgiven me
You say you'll never hurt me
But my heart will not be a ease
Till you tell me that you love me.

I wish I were a butterfly
I'd spread my wings and fly high
Right in to the sky and leave
All you sad people behind.

What can I do?
When I know nothing is true
From the feeling in your heart
To the love that you show
Nothing is real
Not even your tears.

Why am I so scared to tell you?
That when you touch me
I want time to stop
When you hold me
I want you so much
But I fear, if there is a tear,
I may lose you forever.

Just a thought that crossed my heart
That although your not mine
I could never see you with another
As it would kill me forever.

Just one last time, I ask you why?
What did I do wrong, that you felt
The urge to hurt me so bad
That I did not fear if death was around the corner.

I'm a poet not a writer
Who just wants to express
Her inner most desires
To fulfil each dream
Then one day die peacefully.

Never did I ever believe
That life would do this to me
To take something away and
Bring it right back
To give me inspiration
To show me some light
To tell me you've never been alone
I was always by your side.

I stared in to your eyes
Creating a mirror image
I whispered I love you
Till you kissed my lips
I held you so close
I could feel the heat
Moving much closer
I could sense the beat
Feeling you so softly I felt so shy
Till you made sweet love to me,
from day to night.

I looked in to your eyes so deep
And wondered how to tell you
I see your fear, your stress your anxiety
I want to heal you, I want to take your pain
The only way is to look into your eyes
And give you all the love I have in mind.

Once upon a time I had a thought so fine
That if you and I shared more then just our
bodies and minds,
we would truly be a unique pair alive.

When we use to walk
I would look in to your eyes
Wish you were only mine
Till life took a turn
I lost you as you made a run
Without a moment or a backwards glimpse.
You now return after all these years
And it seems as if you just took the wrong turn.

If only you could look in to my eyes
Shine that love brighter then a light
I'd promise to look at you and only you
For the rest of my life.

The softness in your voice
Still echoes in my ears
The tender way you touched me
Still makes me shiver
Life really has turned around
But I still feel close to you then ever.

Why do you bring back the memories?
Create and return a feeling,
I'd locked away
So forever it will stay, in my heart so deep
That nothing and no one
Will be able to retain.

I want you and I don't know who to tell
So I lock my heart with the love I have
And hope that one day, you will care enough to say . . . .
I want the key to your heart forever till the day that we die.

When you tell me that you love me
How am I meant to believe?
That you are the one for me
Not for a second or a minute of passion
But forever and ever.

Although you have changed
Your heart is still in the right place
That it makes me want to be with you
More and more each day.

The grass is green
The sky is blue
The world is so wonderful
I see angels smiling at you.

I dare to see a tear in your eye
But worry my heart will be broken and why?
I dare to speak, I dare to hear
Unless it's what I want for you and I

Once I smiled and forever forgot,
Till the day my darling came in to my life
I began to smile, I learnt to live
To fulfill a dream
Only for you to say . . . .
Well this isn't real.

Our dream
We once shared a dream
Between you and me
That the stars had witnessed
For all these years and still
To share a lifetime, to combine our dreams
And to live happily just you and I.

A dream to fulfill each ambition
That crosses my heart
To ensure everything is set as a goal
I have a dream, I must complete
To see my baby smile at me.

I hold you in my arms
Till morning is night
I whisper sweet things whilst you
Tell me your all mine
We share a kiss, a bond so sweet
That nothing will part us till heaven sends its lift.

When you touched my face
I felt that the moments had never past
For your touch still feels the same
Only your thoughts have changed
Like mine once did.
That I wish I could have you back the way I did.

I really wish
I wish I could tell you
How much it really hurts me
That I broke your heart in tiny pieces
I wish I could hold you, whisper to you
That now and forever
I will never leave you.

Our memories and dreams
That we once shared, feels as if
They are one again
To have you again
To hold you again
Feels truly unreal
That I wish I don't awake.

How can I tell you?
How crazy I am for you
For when you touch me
You make me smile
When you're away
It makes me cry
If this isn't love
Then what is it and why?

I'm waiting for the day you tell me
Your all mine
I will cherish you in my thoughts
Love you, worship you and treasure with you
All my desires in life.

I dream of a world
With you by my side
I know I have nothing to fear
As you are only mine.

All I want is you and only you
I don't know why?
Promise me you will give me you
Days and nights
Your life and your soul but most of all
Promise to stay faithful to me as that's all I want.

A memory from the past
Has come back in to my life
With dreams and desires
We shared once upon a time,
I wish I could hold you
Kiss you and tell you
Baby I promise, I will never make you cry!

I want you more then I could ever imagine
I want to build a life away from all demons
Nothing to fear not even a tear
Just you and I
Imagine forever and ever
Till the day that we die.

Your eyes were only for me
Yet you have forgotten as the love
Has washed away
With the changes in our lives, and the sorrows
In our heart
You will never look at me the way you did.

I have a thought
An inspiration to live
Knowing that one day
You and I
Will become one,
That's why!!!

When we met
There was a sudden ache
I felt in the heart so deep
How did I let you go?
How did I stoop so low?
To leave you my darling
When you wanted me more
I now regret only god knows its faith
That although I want more
I know we will always be friends.

I want more then just a moment
To spend in your arms and feel no pain
To live a life full of amazement
So I'm telling you my darling
A moment is not enough.

I wonder as it hits me
Is it a memory from the past or reality?
That once again
You have stepped in to my life
Without a moment or thought
That I want to hold you tight and tell you
I will never leave your side.

My eyes close in the comfort of your arms
As if to tell me I'm not alone
You hold me so tight
Whisper in my ear
Forever holding you tight.

I close my eyes without a sudden cry
No tears, no shame no water down my face
I sense a feeling so emotional
I did not know how to over come
I searched high and I searched low
But I could not find the cure of my pain

When you touch me
With your words so deep
But ask me a simple question it seems
I did not know how to reply
All I knew was
I had to think twice.

The tear in the river
Caused some sort of shiver
That ran down my spine
That made me cry
To feel such intense pain
I felt my life wasn't worth living.

I have a feeling in my heart
That if it was up to I
I would grab your hand
Run a mile and tell you
My darling, it's just you and I.

You're so unforgettable
That when I close my eyes
I picture your face near mine
I sense you touch
I feel the closeness
As if to remind me
My soul mate, you'll always be mine.

The mirror
When I look in to the mirror
I see you appear
Behind me holding me as I turn to
Look you in the eyes
Your not there
It's all in my mind.

My beauty on my face
Is nothing but a fake mask
That covers my face
Till you my darling, come to mind
That it makes me want to look
Beautiful all the time.

Love hurts and love destroyed
Together with shattered dreams
Was going to be unforgettable till
Your thoughts and memories
Touched each inch of my soul.

My old memories with you
Have become a daily thought of some kind
That without you
I feel my memories are not enough
To live a life.

Today is the day
My heart will speak out to you
Tell you truly
How I feel for you
If then you feel the need to hurt me
It will be my problem and not yours.

My world turned upside down
As I saw you foot steps fade away from me
I could not imagine
What had happened?
Only I wished you'd turn around.

I never want to forget
The feeling that I get
When you hold your head
Against my head
Look in to my eyes and tell me
My darling I'm always by your side.

Nothing and no one
Is unforgettable
Till you wipe them from your
Heart for good
A memory or a part of reality
Everything is so easy to forget
Just like a dream.

I remember how you use to
Make me smile
You'd look me in the eyes
And say I'm here
Surely it's not worth a cry.

As you parted from me
And we lost touch
I lost each emotion
Crossing my heart
I felt surly it wasn't love
Till the day you said
You know it was.

I could never forget you
Not even when I'm with another
I will always have a place for you
Where I will cherish the memories
We once shared
That will help me relive again.

I ask you why?
You say because I don't mind
But is there more
That you can not say
Like forever you want to
Be by my side.

A moment of passion in your arms
Is all I require to tell you
It's time to let go
For you need to find the path
To your destiny, and let
Me come back and live in reality.

I know that
That if you could
You surly would
Take me in your arms for good
Wipe away my fears and my tears
So that I would have no dilemmas.

I sat alone to paint a picture
But didn't even know the colours
in the rainbow
I placed the brush to the paper
To notice your face appear
You looked at me and I looked at you
And straight away I fell in love with you.

You placed your head on my chest
To hear my heart beating slow
You held me close, said "I love you loads"
I smiled and said it's to late
As I need to close my eyes and go.

Your smile creates a miracle
That my heart wants to melt
So much so that I want to say
That without you
Life is a living hell.

The bright sun shone in my eyes
Again to remind me that your still
Watching me with your light eyes
I look in to the sky and see the birds flying high
That I wish I could find you, hold you
Tight and tell you
The sun is nothing and you will shine
Brighter in my life.

My heart is at ease
Only I sense in my sleep
My tears as I weep
In my loneliness without you
I try to fall a sleep.

I wish so much every day
That I could have you back
The time has past, the feelings
have faded away.
But with your return I feel a little
That what your heart once felt was real
Now I have that feeling
But I cant tell you really
How I want you, just the way you did that one day.

I dream of you
Night and day
Just hoping that one day
I fall a sleep
In your arms and our
Dreams are combined together as one.

Why do I feel this need?
That without you life is
Nothing but a dream
Not even a life worth living
That I want you so bad
I can't forget
You, your existence in my life
That I want to share with you
Everything till we have to say farewell.

With you I want a life
A fairy tale of some kind
With happiness surrounding
Each minute of our lives
That we live happily together
Till the day we die.

All I need is a glimpse of you
To begin to tell you how I feel for you
That without you life is worse
Then it has ever been.

I know it's been awhile
But I feel so tired
From telling you how I feel
That you don't seem real
I want you to kneel
Tell me you're here to heal
The love we once shared
That felt like a deal.

The bond that we share
Between our hearts
Is so unreal, it makes me feel
The love we once shared
Is not completely dead
That one day I will make
You feel, what you once felt.

My heart is so crazy
That wherever I look
All I see is you
Why do I feel this?
I can not say
As I was the one to
Let you out of my sight.

Every time my heart beats
It craves for you
Put me to the test
My sweet angel and you will see
I've always been in love with you.

Although you avoid
My existence in your life
I hold your memories close by
I think of you each day
Just wish that you would say . . . .
My darling I know one day you will be mine.

Take my heart and you will see
My life revolves round you
That my hopes, my dreams
Are all pinned on you
You are truly the one
That each breath of mine is tied to.

This world is so wonderful
But without you it feels so dull
Just the presence of you is all I want
For the world to look wonderful.

All my love, from deep within my soul
Is what I want to give you alone
Have you my entire life
Through happiness and sadness
I will be by your side.

A wonderful dream
I had of you
Where you held my hand
Told me you are only mine
Till I woke up and saw it was a lie.

I have a emotion, deep in the heart
That comes out as tears on my face
I wish I could tell you
How much it really hurts me
To not have you in front of my eyes.

I wish you could feel
What I feel and have me
Close to your heart for real
Share each thought like a fantasy
on a boat,
without any rocks so we happily float.

I want to . . . .
I want to make sweet love to you
Day and night
Hold you in my arms so tight
Fall asleep and never want to cry
Spend the rest of our lives
Together without a fright.

I'm sorry, I said it that way
It's a shame I felt that way
But if I hadn't
You wouldn't have walked away
I need you to go
So I can fold
The memories we shared away for good.

I see myself in a field full of grass
Standing alone
Not knowing at all
What the future holds
That I want to run
Further then I can from the past.

My voice did not reach you
In the darkness of the night
Was it that you ignored me?
As it felt like a fright
I long to tell you
That I really love you
But it's a pity my voice can not reach you.

I don't know anymore
What true love is all about?
With you forgetting
My memories are fading
That I feel my happiness is in me being alone.

What is it about me?
That makes you want to hurt me
My heart is not healing
Knowing and once feeling
Your still not willing to reveal
Your hearts true feelings.

My last moment s spent with you
I held you and told you
Please don't let me go, for if you do
This heart may never love again
To part from you and never to ever feel
The closeness, we once shared.

I can smell your essence as I walk down the road
I turn around and you're nowhere to be found
I feel you're there somewhere beside me,
Hiding away, worried
I might change you essence with my beauty.

I sit here alone
Knowing it all
That happiness will never
Even touch my soul
That the man of my dreams
Will never be by my side
Not even the day that I die.

MUM!

When I think about what to say to you

I wonder where to begin to start to tell you

What I need to . . . .

And I really get lost for words

You're then when I'm hurt,

You're there when I'm happy

People say when you cry you cry alone

But when you smile the world smiles with you

But with you it all different

I guess that's why they call you a Mother

You comfort me through my sorrows and enjoy

Every moment of my happiness.

I sometimes wish I'd never grown up,

Still wish you could wrap me in your arms, hold

me tight, wipe my tears and say don't fear as I am here.

But then I open my eyes and see my son and it

Reminds me of what you have done for me,

IT'S MY TURN NOW!

I sometimes wish I could show you tell you

How much I appreciate what you've done

But when I think of what to say

AGAIN . . . .

I'm lost as there is no way of repaying you!